. . . IF YOU LIVED WITH
THE HOPI

BY ANNE KAMMA

ILLUSTRATED BY LINDA GARDNER

SCHOLASTIC INC.

NEW YORK   TORONTO   LONDON   AUCKLAND

SYDNEY   MEXICO CITY   NEW DELHI   HONG KONG

FOR MY FATHER, IN LOVING MEMORY

ACKNOWLEDGMENTS

With grateful thanks to the staff at the Smithsonian National Museum of the American Indian; the Hopi Cultural Preservation Office; the Bancroft Public Library in Salem, New York; the New York Public Library; Greg Markee at the Museum of Northern Arizona; Arlene Hirschfelder, Native American studies consultant; Catherine M. Cameron, Department of Anthropology, University of Colorado; Grace Goodman; Phil Israel; Jane Kaufman; Karen Krugman; and Harry Orlyk; my wonderful editor, Eva Moore; and Ellen Levine, for her insightful suggestions in reviewing the manuscript. Special mention should be made of the book *Hopi*, written by Susanne and Jake Page at the request of the Hopi themselves. It proved an invaluable resource. The quotations about the blue corn legend are from Albert Yava's book *Big Falling Snow* (Albuquerque: University of New Mexico Press, 1978).

ISBN 0-590-39726-5

Book design by Cristina Costantino and Laurie Williams

12 11 10 9 8 7 6 5 4 3 2   9/9 0 1 2 3 4/0

Printed in the U.S.A.
First Scholastic printing, November 1999

CONTENTS

Introduction

The first Spanish explorers came to North America more than five hundred years ago. When they arrived, there were already many Native Americans living here — millions of them, some historians say.

The Native Americans were divided into different tribes. Each tribe had its own language and its own way of living.

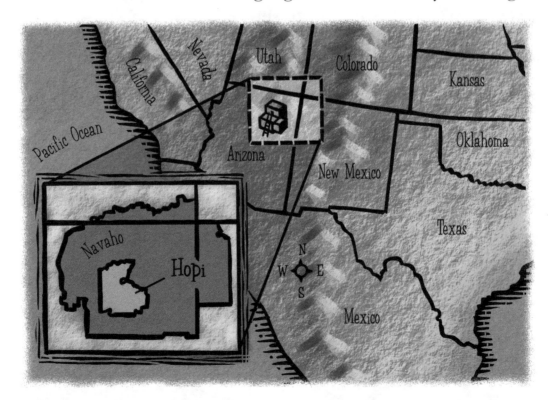

Some hunted whales. Some hunted buffalo. Some were farmers. Many tribes never even met each other because they lived so far apart.

This book is about the Hopi tribe. They lived in the high desert of Arizona, one hundred miles east of the Grand Canyon.

Like many other Native American tribes of the southwestern United States, the Hopi were known as Pueblo Indians. *Pueblo* is the Spanish word for "village." And all these Indians lived in villages, with houses made of stone and clay.

Hopi means "the peaceful and wise people." They believed that it was best to try to live in peace and harmony with the world around them.

The Hopi still live in the same place they have lived for more than a thousand years. They were never forced to leave their land the way most other Indian tribes were, and some of their ancient villages are standing today. In fact, if you wanted to visit the oldest town in America where people still live, you would go to Oraibi, in the land of the Hopi.

Would you live in a tepee?

No. The Hopi were farmers, not hunters. They stayed in one place and built their villages near their fields and springs.

It was the Plains Indians who lived in tepees. They were hunters and had to follow the buffalo herds. So they needed houses they could fold up and carry with them.

Hopi houses were made of stone and clay and had flat roofs. They looked like apartment buildings and were often two or three stories high. Nobody lived on the ground floor. That was used for storing things.

To enter your house, you climbed up a ladder. Then you walked across the roof and in the front door.

Your house was a busy place. Women ground corn, wove baskets, and cooked food, all inside if the weather was bad. In good weather, everyone worked, ate, and sometimes even slept outside on the flat roof. The smell of corn

pudding or stew with wild onions filled the air. When you were ready for supper, everyone sat on the floor and ate out of a big clay pot. The Hopi did not use dining tables or chairs.

Who would live in your house?

Your house would be full of relatives. There would be your sisters and your brothers, and your mother and your father, and lots of other relatives.

Hopi women didn't leave their home when they got married, because a house belonged to all the women who lived in it. It was the husbands who moved in with them.

So you would also be living with your aunts and uncles and cousins and great-aunts and great-uncles.

Your grandmother was the head of the household so, of course, she and your grandfather would live there, too.

You might have ten, fifteen, or even twenty relatives living with you! They would all be working together so that everyone was taken care of.

What happened if your house got too crowded?

Sometimes there were so many people living in your house that you ran out of room. Then something had to be done.

One thing was certain: You would never have to leave and have no place to go. The Hopi had a much better way of solving the problem: They added more rooms.

It didn't cost anything to make your house bigger. All it took was hard work. You just went outside the village and gathered what you needed. You'd get stones and clay for making the walls and floor. And you'd get grass, brush, and mud for making the roof.

There was only one thing that was hard to get: the wooden beams needed for holding up the roof. That was because the Hopi had no forests near their villages. It took the men days to haul the heavy tree trunks down from Black Mesa forests that were miles away.

When all the materials were ready, everyone helped to build the new rooms. If your house was *really* crowded, you might have to add a whole extra story.

How would you keep warm?

You didn't worry about keeping warm, even during the coldest winter.

You could make a fire with sticks from juniper and greasewood bushes, which you'd gather from the desert. There was a rule: Never return home empty-handed. By the time everyone had brought a few sticks, there'd be a nice little pile of wood for the fire.

Still, there wasn't enough wood around to keep the houses warm all winter. But the Hopi had discovered another way to keep warm: coal. Coal looks like a black rock, but it burns and produces heat. The Hopi were among the first people in the world to use coal for heating their homes.

The coal lay in the ground near the surface, and there was plenty of it. You'd dig it out by hand and carry it back to your house.

The ancient Hopi used a lot of coal. One village, called Awatovi, is believed to have burned 450 pounds a day!

Who would take care of you?

First, of course, there would be your mother, who would love you and take care of you.

But your mother's sisters — your aunts — would also take care of you. They would live in your house with you. They would treat you like one of their own children and help raise you. You'd call them *ngú u*, which is the Hopi word for "mother."

If something should ever happen to your mother, your aunts would take over your mother's job of raising you. And, of course, they would get lots of help from your father, your grandparents, and other people in your clan.

Badger

Butterfly

What was a clan?

A clan was made up of people who were related to you through your mother's female ancestors. A clan might have hundreds of people in it.

Everyone belonged to a clan. The minute you were born, you would be a member of your mother's clan. Maybe it would be the Snake Clan or the Greasewood Clan. Maybe it would be the Sun Clan or one of the many other Hopi clans.

When you grew up, you'd have to make sure that the person you wanted to marry was from a different clan. Otherwise you wouldn't be allowed to get married.

Why was a clan so important?

A clan was like a big family. Each clan had its own special history of how it arrived in the land of the Hopi, and its

Bear

Spider

Snake

Blue Flute

Eagle

Cloud

Coyote

own special duties. To know your clan was to know where you came from and where you belonged.

It was very important to be part of a clan. If you were in trouble, members of your clan helped out. If you traveled to another Hopi village, you could visit clan members there.

Clans controlled all the farmland. Each clan had its own piece of land, which was divided up among the women of the clan. If you were a girl, you'd grow up to own land from your clan.

Each clan also had its own religious ceremonies. These clan ceremonies were thought to have special powers to help all the Hopi people.

How would you get your name?

You wouldn't have just one name. You'd have different names at different times in your life.

When you were born, you'd get your first name at the naming ceremony. Your name would show which clan your father belonged to. If he was from the Bear Clan, you might be called *Hontoechi*, which means "bear moccasins." If your father was from the Water Clan, they might call you *Batoti*, which means "water all over."

But you would not have a last name. The Hopi never used them.

When you were six years old, you would be given a new name in a religious ceremony. And you'd get another name when you became an adult. That is the name you would keep for the rest of your life.

But there would be one last name: a silent name.

It would be given to you when you died. The name would never be spoken. The funeral attendant would only think it. So only she and your spirit would ever know what it was.

That is the name you would take with you to your new spirit home.

When would you first go outside?

As soon as a baby was born, blankets were hung over the windows and entrances. No sunlight was allowed to shine on the mother and the new baby. Otherwise, the Hopi believed, great harm would come to them both.

So when you were born, you stayed indoors for the first nineteen days.

But the twentieth day was different. Before the sun rose, your grandmother gave you a name at the sacred naming ceremony. Your father, meanwhile, was outside watching for the sunrise. At just the right moment, he gave a signal.

Now was the time for you to be taken outside.

Your grandmother would lift you up toward the sun. And as the first rays of sun touched your face, you were presented to Tawa, the sun god and great giver of life.

What clothes would you wear?

Children wore the same kind of clothes as adults.

If you were a girl, you'd wear a *manta*. It looked like a dress, but it was really a black cotton blanket wrapped around you and fastened together on your right shoulder. You would tie a sash around your waist to keep the *manta* in place.

If you were a boy, you'd wear a breechcloth or kilt. If you got cold, you'd wear loose pants and a shirt.

Most of your clothes were made out of cotton, not deer-skin. There were very few deer around to hunt, but the Hopi had plenty of cotton. They grew it themselves.

Everyone wore leggings in cold weather. Sometimes you wore sandals and sometimes moccasins. The sandals were made from the yucca plant, and the moccasins were made of deerskin.

In winter, if you were really cold, you might wear a blanket made of strips of rabbit skin woven together.

In summer, when it was warm, young children usually wore nothing at all.

Where would you find water?

The Hopi didn't have any lakes or rivers, so you couldn't go there to get water. But they did have springs. A spring is a place where water comes out of the ground.

Springs were very important. The Hopi could not have lived in the desert without them.

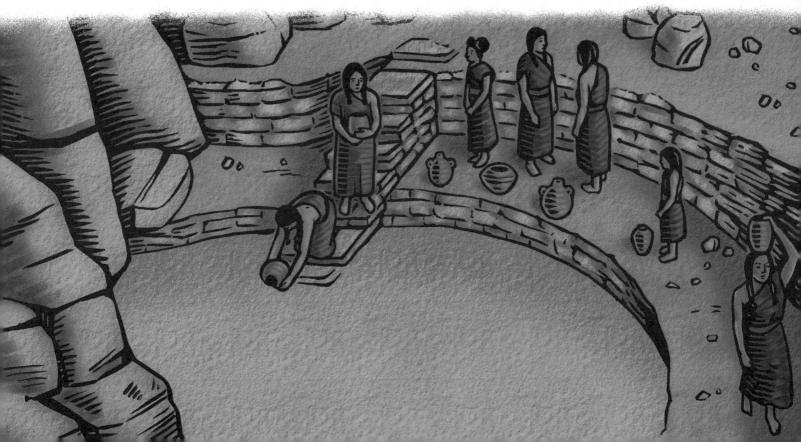

The springs were located at the bottom of the mesas where the Hopi lived. A mesa is a small, flat-topped mountain.

When it rained or snowed, the mesa acted like a giant sponge. The water seeped into the mesa and then very slowly made its way down. It took almost two years for the water to reach the bottom.

Only a little water trickled out into the open at one time. So the Hopi dug holes around the springs to collect the water.

This is where you went to get your water for drinking and cooking and for watering your small vegetable garden. This is also where you bathed, even in the winter — and the colder the better! For the Hopi believed that cold baths helped you live longer.

Why did the Hopi carve holes in the mesa rock?

The Hopi needed more water than they could get from their springs. They knew that in the desert, every drop counted. So each family had a deep, wide hole, called a cistern, which had been carved out of the mesa rock.

The cistern was a place for storing extra water for your family. In the summer it filled with rainwater. In the winter it filled with melting snow. Sometimes you and your family would pack lots of extra snow around the cistern just to make sure it filled up.

Carving a cistern out of the rock was very hard work. One Hopi man, Don Talayesva, remembers his grand-father talking about the cistern he had carved long ago. His grandfather had made it when he got married so that his children and grandchildren would never go thirsty.

What would you eat?

You would eat corn every day! The Hopi grew many different kinds of corn — yellow, white, blue, speckled, and red.

At harvest time, you'd eat fresh roasted corn on the cob. But most of the time your food would be made from ground-up dry corn, called cornmeal.

If you think that sounds boring, you'd be wrong. The Hopi could make just about anything from cornmeal. One of their favorites was *piki* (PEEK-ee) bread, a kind of pancake made with blue cornmeal. They made other breads and delicious soups, porridges, and dumplings — even snacks and desserts.

You would also eat lots of squash and beans. And you'd eat wild plants and seeds, which you'd help your mother gather in the desert.

In the summer there were wild potatoes and berries. In the fall there were piñon nuts. Piñon nuts were one of the Hopi's favorite treats. In the springtime, you would eat wild greens, like the Rocky Mountain beeweed, which tasted just like spinach.

The Hopi ate very little meat. Sometimes you had rabbit and once in a while some deer or antelope meat.

But you wouldn't eat fish. Can you guess why?

How could corn grow in the desert?

If the Hopi had tried to plant the kind of corn you find today in Kansas or Iowa, they wouldn't have been able to make it grow.

But the Hopi had a special kind of corn: desert corn. This corn had been grown by their ancestors for thousands of years. It had very long roots — sometimes as long as fifteen feet — so it could reach down to the moisture that was found deep in the ground.

The long roots also helped in another important way. They kept the plant from being blown away by the strong desert winds.

Hopi corn

Iowa corn

moist soil

Where did the Hopi plant their corn?

The Hopi planted most of their corn seeds near dry streambeds, called washes.

Once in a while there would be a violent rainstorm. Then the water would rush down the mesas and into the washes. There would usually be so much water that some of it would overflow onto the cornfields.

The Hopi also discovered another place to plant their corn: the sand dunes. Now, you might think that a dune is completely dry, but it actually holds a lot of water.

How would you keep the corn from spoiling?

One of the best ways to keep food from spoiling is to dry it. All you need is hot, dry air, and the Hopi had plenty of that.

After a harvest, everyone husked the corn and spread the corncobs out on their roofs. When the corncobs were completely dry, they were taken inside the house and stacked on shelves. Dry corn lasted for years.

When you were ready to cook, you scraped the kernels off the corncob. Then you ground the kernels into corn-meal on special grinding stones, called *metates*.

What was a sun watcher?

The Hopi didn't need a calendar to tell them when to start planting their seeds or celebrate their religious ceremonies. They just asked their sun watcher.

When the sun rose at a certain spot on the horizon, the sun watcher knew it was time to plant the seeds. When it rose at different spots, he knew it was time for the Snake Dance ceremony or the Home Dance.

It was very important to plant your seeds at the right time. Planting at the wrong time could mean disaster for everyone in your village. That was because Hopi corn took a long time to ripen. And the growing season in the desert is short. So you had to know just when to start.

If you planted the seeds too early, the spring frost might kill the young shoots. If you planted the seeds too late, the corn might not ripen in time before the cold weather set in. Then there would be no harvest and no food.

So it was very important to listen to the sun watcher.

August was the time for the sacred Snake Dance.

What happened if it didn't rain?

If it didn't rain, the plants couldn't grow. Then everyone worried about what they were going to eat.

The Hopi usually had a two- or three-year supply of corn stored away. It was their insurance.

But once in a while a drought lasted for years. Then everyone ran out of corn and had to eat wild plants and seeds.

It was very hard to find enough wild plants for everyone to live on. But there was one plant that grew everywhere: a tall grass called dropseed. If you put a cloth under it and shook it, lots of seeds would fall to the ground. The seeds were ground up into meal. It didn't taste as good as cornmeal, but it kept you from starving.

Would you ever have to leave your home?

If the drought lasted too long, there was only one thing to do to keep from dying: Everyone would have to leave.

You might have to walk more than 200 miles to live with other Pueblo Indians along the Rio Grande River. There, you and your family would work hard just to get enough food to eat. It would be a terrible time.

But one day a wonderful thing would happen: The rain would return. Then you and your family and everyone from your village could go back home.

What did girls have to learn?

Hopi men and women had different jobs to do. So girls learned their mothers' work.

You'd have to learn to repair the walls of your house. It was the women's job to replace missing stones and plaster the walls with clay. You'd also learn how to make pottery and baskets. But you wouldn't learn how to weave and sew — that was the men's job.

Women did all the cooking. Before dried corn was cooked, it had to be ground into cornmeal. So women spent many hours a day at their *metates*, the grinding stones.

Grinding took a lot of strength because dry corn was very hard. If you were a girl, you would learn how to grind a little at a time so that your arms could get stronger and stronger.

While you were grinding corn, you'd have plenty of time to talk with your mother and your sister working next to you. And you'd have plenty of time to sing the beautiful songs that Hopi women sang while they worked.

What did boys have to learn?

All Hopi men were farmers, so if you were a boy you would learn how to be one, too. You'd learn how to grow corn, beans, squash, and cotton.

You'd also learn how to put on the religious ceremonies of your clan. And you'd learn how to spin cotton, weave, and sew clothes. That, too, was the men's job.

When you were six years old, you started helping your father in the fields. He would show you how to plant seeds deep in the ground with a digging stick. And he would teach you how to build windbreaks with stones and brush to protect the young plants from the blowing sand.

You also learned how to kill mice and rats, even if you had to dig them out of their holes first. If you didn't, they might eat the crops. At harvest time you'd have to hoot and holler to chase off the crows.

Every boy learned how to hunt rabbits with a bow and arrow. Hunting kept the rabbits from eating the crops. And it meant delicious rabbit stew for dinner!

What was the "Hopi Way"?

The Hopi believed it was very important to have a good heart. Their religion taught them so.

To be helpful and kind to others, to live in harmony with the world — that was the Hopi Way.

Thoughts were believed to have strong powers. Bad thoughts, such as feeling mean or selfish, could make you sick or harm others.

Good thoughts had the power to help. And if many people *together* had good thoughts, then those powers were so strong they could help bring rain and a good harvest. This, the Hopi believed, was especially true of group prayers.

So if you had mean or sad thoughts one day, you would not join in religious ceremonies. You would wait until those thoughts were gone. Otherwise you might keep the prayers from working.

What was the Hopi religion?

The Hopi believed everything in nature had its own sacred spirit — people, animals, plants, even rocks and clouds.

They also believed in great spirits, sometimes called gods. Some of the most important gods were Sósqtuknang and Tawa, who created the world, and Kokyang Wuuti (or Spider Woman), who many Hopi believed created the first human beings.

The Hopi believed that if they lived in harmony with the spirits, they would be rewarded — plenty of rain for the crops and a good life for their people. But to live in harmony you had to have what they called a "good heart." That meant being truthful and kind and trying to live in peace with your neighbors. It also meant honoring the spirits with prayers and performing all the sacred ceremonies throughout the year.

The Hopi believed that their ceremonies were important for everybody, not just the Hopi. They believed that their ceremonies were necessary to keep the whole world in balance.

Who were the kachinas?

The kachinas (kuh-CHEE-nahs) were the Hopi's special protectors.

They were not gods but powerful spirits who, the Hopi believed, came to their village every year to help them. If the Hopi had performed their religious ceremonies well and had good hearts, the kachinas would help bring rain and a good harvest.

At kachina ceremonies, men dressed as kachina spirits. They wore masks that covered their heads and sang and danced in the sacred ceremonies. The Hopi believed that when the men performed these rituals, their human spirits were replaced by the actual spirits of the kachinas.

Most kachinas were kind and often gave out presents to the children. But there were also a few scary ones. (See pages 47–48.)

With more than 200 different kachinas, it wasn't easy to learn who they all were. That's why you might be given kachina dolls like these to help you remember.

Leader

Pour Water Woman

Butterfly Maiden

Cloud-Bringing

Flute

What was a kiva?

A kiva (KEY-va) was a sacred room that was often under-ground. To enter, you climbed through a hole in the roof and down a ladder.

The kiva was a very important place in the village. This was where the men planned all the religious ceremonies, prayed, and discussed governing the village.

If you were a boy, you would go there to learn about the Hopi religion. You would be taught all the songs and dances, the prayers and the secret ceremonies. You would be taught how to make kachina masks and costumes. And you would learn the sacred history of the Hopi people.

As you got older, you'd spend more and more time with the men in the kiva.

There was a lot to learn, because these ceremonies had to be performed just the right way. Otherwise, the Hopi believed, they wouldn't work.

Would you have fun in the kiva?

Yes. Sometimes you went to the kiva just to relax and sing and tell stories. The Hopi loved to sing and make up new songs.

The Hopi were also wonderful storytellers. You learned the stories by hearing them over and over again. Then one day *you* might become the storyteller.

While you listened to the stories, you would probably weave or sew. The Hopi liked to work. And the men made everybody's clothing — even the beautiful white robes that Hopi brides wore on their wedding day.

What happened if you did something bad?

Hopi children were raised with lots of love and patience. So most of the time it wasn't necessary to punish them.

If you did do something bad, like neglecting your work or hitting someone, your father didn't punish you.

Your uncle did.

He might take you from house to house and pour cold water on you while your relatives watched. You'd be so ashamed that you'd probably never do the bad thing again!

What if you were really, really bad?

Every Hopi child was told what would happen if you continued to be *really* bad: The ogre kachinas, who ate bad children and came to the village once a year, would come knocking at your door!

The terrifying monsters would call out all the bad things you had done. You'd stand there shaking, looking at their big fangs and their basket for carrying you away for their supper.

But your family would refuse to hand you over.

They would plead with the kachinas, telling them about all the *good* things you had done. Your family would offer the kachinas rabbit meat and *piki* bread to eat instead. And they would promise that you would be good.

Finally convinced, the ogre kachinas would move on down the street to knock on another door and call out the name of another misbehaving child.

If you were a young child, you wouldn't know that they were really villagers dressed up like kachinas.

Would you go to school?

Hopi children learned by doing what everyone around them was doing. They didn't have to go to a school the way children do today.

Your teachers were your parents, grandparents, aunts and uncles, sisters and brothers, and other clan members. They taught you everything you needed to know — how to farm, grind corn, hunt rabbits, make pottery, build your house, and gather wild plants.

You learned Hopi history by listening to storytellers, like those who came to your house on winter evenings after everyone had finished their supper.

The Hopi used their memories to preserve important information, just as we use books and computers today. They did not have a written language or books. You learned by hearing something told many times. After a while, you got to know the information so well that you could teach it to someone else.

Did children have to work?

Yes. Everyone, even young children, helped with the work. There were no stores where you could buy things, so people had to make everything themselves: shoes, clothes, blankets, axes — even cooking pots and ovens. That took a lot of time.

When you were little, you started out by helping your mother with the cooking and the cleaning.

You also helped bring in firewood. And you went out into the desert with your mother or your aunt to pick berries and gather wild plants for food and medicines.

Were boys more important than girls?

No. Unlike most societies, the Hopi thought boys and girls were equally important, just as they did men and women.

Hopi girls knew that when they grew up they would own the land, the springs, the houses, and the food. They would even own the seeds that were planted each spring in the fields. They would cook and take care of the house and children.

They would also make the pottery and baskets that the men traded with other Indian tribes. Hopi women were famous for their beautiful pottery. And trade brought the Hopi many things they wanted — like buckskin, parrot feathers, sweet agave plants, seashells, and turquoise.

Hopi men performed all the religious ceremonies. They grew all the food. And they defended their village if it was attacked. The men thought that what the women did was just as important as what they did.

What games would you play?

Hopi children loved team sports.

You'd run races and play lots of ball games. And you'd have dart-throwing contests with darts made of corncobs and feathers. To the Hopi, the fun was in the game, not in who won. So you'd probably not bother keeping score.

Some games, like archery, were thought to have sacred powers to bring rain. So when you shot your arrow at a rolling hoop, you'd not only be having fun, you'd be helping the crops grow!

Everyone loved a game that was much like our field hockey. The ball was made of buckskin stuffed with deer hair. You'd hit the ball with curved sticks. There was no time limit on the game, so you could play as long as you liked. If the moon was bright, you might go on playing after it got dark.

What would you do in the winter?

Winter was the time for stories.

In the evening, your family would gather around the storyteller. Perhaps he would tell you the story of the child who turned into an owl. Perhaps it would be a story about Hopi history.

A storyteller was never allowed to change anything in the story. The Hopi believed that all stories had to be told just exactly the way they had been told for hundreds of years.

There was no farmwork to do, so the men and boys had plenty of time to spend in the kiva. They would spin cotton, weave, sew clothes, and make moccasins and kachina dolls.

One of your jobs during the winter was to help guard the corn from the mice. Otherwise there might not be anything left for your family to eat. And sometimes you'd help take the dry corncobs off the shelves and put them out on the roof to "sunbathe." That was how the Hopi got rid of some of the corn-eating insects.

How would you get the latest news?

Each village had a town crier. It was his job to shout out the latest news. You would hear him in the early morning or during supper time, when everyone was sure to be at home.

"Haliksa-I" he would cry from the highest rooftop. "Listen! This is how it is!"

First he would say a prayer. Then he would bring the news. He might tell you that everyone was invited to a breakfast celebrating somebody's new baby. Or he might welcome visitors from another village.

If you some had extra *piki* bread or meat that you wanted to trade, the crier would announce it. And when the pools that held the springwater got filled up with mud and it was time for the village to clean them out, the crier would let you know that, too.

Sometimes, though, he wouldn't call out any news. He would just sing an ancient Hopi song while everyone sat and listened.

Did Hopi parents ever get divorced?

Yes. Hopi parents sometimes got divorced. If a woman didn't want to be married anymore, she would put her husband's belongings outside the house. That meant they were divorced. If a man didn't want to be married anymore, he would move out of the house. That also meant they were divorced.

If your parents got divorced, you would stay with your mother. You wouldn't lose your home, because a Hopi house always belonged to the women who lived in it.

Your father would go back home to live in his mother's house and help her farm her land. But he would not be far away.

Everyone living in your household — aunts, uncles, grandparents, and cousins — would help out. Even your mother's fields would be planted and harvested, because your uncles and other members of your mother's clan would take over your father's work. That way you and your mother and sisters and brothers would be sure to have food to eat.

And you'd still have a houseful of caring relatives.

Would you go on an eagle-gathering trip?

If you were a boy, you might be chosen to go on an eagle-gathering trip.

A village clan had its own eagle grounds. In the late spring, when the hatchling eagles were still too young to fly, your group would search the cliffs. The Hopi believed that if their prayers had been answered, you would find a nest with a young eagle in it.

Then you would be lowered by a rope over the rim of the cliff. Sometimes the cliffs were hundreds of feet high! When you reached the nest below, you would tie a rope around the struggling eagle's foot.

After you were both pulled back up safely, the eagle would be taken back to your village. If it had been a good eagle-gathering year, there might already be other eagles perched on the roofs high above the village.

Why was the eagle important to the Hopi?

The Hopi believed that everything in nature had a spirit. The spirit of the eagle was especially important because it was a messenger to the gods.

A young eagle that had never hunted was pure, they thought, so it would always tell the truth. And its strong eyes made it a good observer.

The Hopi wanted the eagle to sit high on a roof so that it could watch everyone in the village. They treated the captured eagle with great respect. They named it in a special naming ceremony. They said prayers and gave it special foods and toys.

The Hopi wanted the eagle to see that they had lived good lives and had performed all their religious duties. Then later, when the eagle died, its spirit would tell the gods. The gods would bring on the rain. And the Hopi would stay strong.

The eagle was also very important to the Hopi because its feathers were used to make *pahos*, or prayer feathers. The feathers were tied to painted and carved sticks with cotton yarn. The Hopi used the *pahos* for many of the prayers they said every day.

Pahos are still used today, just as they were a long time ago.

Where did the Hopi get their salt?

Once a year a small group of men made a long, dangerous journey.

First they traveled for days across the desert until they reached the Grand Canyon. Then they climbed down the steep cliffs to the canyon floor. It was here, at a sacred place, that they gathered their salt.

Spanish explorers called crossing this desert "the journey of death." So how did the Hopi, who didn't even have horses, do it?

First of all, the Hopi were famous runners. They moved so fast that the trip took less time. But they also had a trick. When the men started out on their trip, Hopi women sometimes walked with them part of the way, carrying gourds full of water. These gourds were buried at spots along the trail. The women then went back to the village.

When the men returned with the salt, they knew that there would be water waiting for them on the last part of the trip. All they had to do was dig up the gourds.

Why didn't the Hopi mind living in the desert?

The Hopi believed that it was their destiny to live in the desert. Their religion taught them so. It taught them that after the first human beings climbed up from the underworld into this world, everyone was divided up into tribes.

Different villages had different ways of telling what happened next. Some Hopi believed that the mockingbird told each new tribe to choose a symbolic ear of corn. The mockingbird explained that the corn would reveal their destiny. If you chose the yellow corn, for example, it would bring you great enjoyment but a short life.

The Navajo began by taking the yellow corn, and the Comanches took the red corn. The Utes took the flint corn. Soon everyone was grabbing corn. Only the Hopi watched and did nothing. Finally just one corn was left: the short blue corn, which nobody wanted. The Hopi leader picked it up and said, "Well, this ear is mine. It means we will have to work hard, but we will live long, full lives."

All the new tribes started looking around for places to live. After wandering a long time, the Hopi arrived at the three mesas in the desert. There they met Masauwu, god of the upper world and death, who owned the land. He gave them permission to stay. The Hopi had found their home.

The Hopi believed that the spirits would watch over them in their new home if they worked hard and led good lives. One Hopi story tells how the first settlers looked around at their new homeland and said, "Life will be hard in this place, but no one will envy us. No one will try to take our land away. This is the place where we will stay."

What happened when the Hopi and the Spanish first met?

The Spanish came to Arizona looking for gold. But their soldiers found no gold. All they found were Indian villages.

In 1540, Pedro de Tobar and his soldiers reached the land of the Hopi. It was the first time the Hopi had ever seen white men or horses. They made a line of sacred cornmeal in the sand, telling the intruders not to cross it.

But the Spanish attacked. The Hopi were no match for soldiers with guns, metal armor, and frightening horses. So the Hopi brought gifts to show that they wanted to live in peace.

Tobar accepted the offering of corn, cloth, skins, and piñon nuts. And because the Hopi had no gold, he and his soldiers left.

How did the Spanish treat the Indians?

Although the Indians had no gold, the Spanish soon decided to take something else — their land. The Spanish said that all the Indian lands now belonged to Spain.

The Spanish treated the Pueblo Indians terribly — especially those living along the Rio Grande River. They stole their food and blankets and killed anyone who resisted. Many Indians were forced to work as slaves.

Others died from smallpox and other new diseases brought by the Spanish.

The Hopi, however, were saved by the desert. Their land was so poor that not even the Spanish wanted to settle there.

So long as the Spanish wanted only land, the Hopi were safe. But in 1629 the Spanish priests arrived. They believed it was better for the Hopi to give up their religion and become Catholic.

The priests sometimes used cruel methods. They punished those caught practicing the Hopi religion: Some Hopi were whipped or tortured. Some were even killed.

Still, the Spanish priests could not make the Hopi give up their ancient religion. Only a few of the Indians converted to Catholicism; the rest practiced their religion in secret.

Did the Hopi ever fight the Spanish?

Yes. In 1680, the Hopi decided it was time to fight. Led by a Tewa chief named Popé, the Hopi joined with all the other Pueblo tribes and attacked the Spanish.

They drove the Spanish out of their villages, destroyed the mission churches, and killed many of the priests. Thousands of Pueblo warriors fought the Spanish soldiers — and won. The Spanish were forced to flee in disgrace.

But the Hopi were afraid that Spanish soldiers might one day return and punish them. So they did two things. First, they invited other Indians fleeing the Spanish to come live with them. That way there would be more warriors to help them fight. The Hopi also moved their villages up to the top of the mesas, where it was harder for the Spanish to attack them.

The plan worked. Spanish attacks failed, and the Hopi were left alone.

Did other Indian tribes attack the Hopi?

Yes. Even though the Hopi tried to live in peace with other tribes, they did get attacked by other Indians. Sometimes Apache, Ute, and Navajo bands on horseback raided Hopi villages and stole their corn. Sometimes they captured Hopi women and children and sold them as slaves to the Spanish and the Mexicans. If you were sold as a slave, you might never see your home again.

By 1850, Navajo raids were so bad that a group of Hopi leaders traveled to Santa Fe to ask the United States military for help. But the raids, which also attacked white settlers, continued. Not until 1863, when American forces led by the famous mountain man Kit Carson defeated the Navajo, did most of the raids on Hopi villages finally end.

Did the Americans treat the Hopi better?

When the Americans won the Mexican-American War in 1848, the land of the Hopi became part of the United States.

At first, the Americans left the Hopi alone. Sometimes they even helped them, as when American troops stopped the Navajo raids on Hopi villages.

Later, when the Hopi complained that white settlers had moved onto their land, President Chester A. Arthur created a Hopi reservation. A reservation is land that the U.S. government sets aside for Indian tribes to use.

The reservation *did* keep out the white settlers. But the Hopi lost all their ancestral land that was outside the reservation. And they had to share the reservation with the Navajo.

Worst of all, the government at that time thought all Indians were uncivilized. It wanted to make the Hopi stop living like Hopi and start living like white Americans.

Why didn't the Hopi want to send their children to government schools?

When the U.S. government built the first Hopi schools in the late 1800s, it wanted to teach Hopi children to act like white Americans.

Some of the schools were built so far away that children couldn't go home after classes. They had to live at these boarding schools. The government set up boarding schools because it thought if you were away from home, your family couldn't teach you Indian ways.

Many Hopi refused to send their children to these schools. Some tried to hide their children when the troops came looking for them. If a child was found, the troops took him or her away and put the child's father in jail.

The Hopi were very upset about the government schools. They wanted their children to live at home. Some parents did want their children to learn English and new skills. But nobody wanted schools that tried to destroy the Hopi culture.

How were children treated at the Indian boarding schools?

Indian boarding schools were very strict. They thought it was their duty to get rid of your Indian ways, no matter what tribe you came from.

Only English was allowed. If they caught you speaking in your own language, you were punished — maybe even whipped.

Your clothes were taken from you when you arrived. You were given American-style clothes and an American-style haircut.

You were forbidden to practice your own religion, and you were forced to go to church. You were called by an American name instead of your own name.

Because the boarding schools were so far away, you couldn't see your family very often. Some children were kept at the boarding school for a very long time. So long, in fact, that they did forget some of their own ways. One girl who returned home for a visit refused to wear the Hopi clothes her brother had woven for her. She no longer felt at ease with her own family.

This was a sad time for everyone.

Do the Hopi live differently today?

For many years, the United States government wanted to change the Hopi way of life. It tried to keep the Hopi from practicing their religion. It tried to force them to give up their ancient way of owning land. It made Hopi parents send their children away to school. And it wouldn't let the Hopi govern themselves.

But under President Franklin D. Roosevelt, the government began to change. In 1934, the Indian Reorganization Act was passed. This new law said that the government should help protect Indian traditions, not try to destroy them. It also said that Indians had a right to their own land and to more self-government.

The law did not solve all the problems between the Hopi and the government. It was just the beginning. But today, more than sixty years later, Hopi children can go to nearby schools — schools that teach pride in their Hopi heritage, as well as modern skills.

The Hopi no longer live the way their ancestors did. Many work outside the reservation. Some men don't farm anymore. And the Hopi don't have to make everything themselves, because they can go to stores to buy what they need. They continue to make their beautiful pottery and jewelry and baskets. But they also have cars and TVs and videos, just as other Americans do. And many live in modern houses.

The Hopi still honor their ancient traditions. Clans are strong. If you were to visit a Hopi village today, you might hear the ancient songs and see the ancient dances. And the Hopi still teach their children how important it is to try and live in peace and cooperation, the Hopi Way.